CHAKRA MEDICINE

haiku

CHAKRA MEDICINE

haiku

Lisa Rae Cunningham

Walk In Beauty
Los Angeles
2023

Copyright © 2023 by Lisa Rae Cunningham

All rights reserved. Published in California
by Walk In Beauty. Venice + Santa Monica

ISBN 979-8-218-13500-3

for my son

Contents

Muladhara 11
Chakra One: Earth

Svadhisthana 29
Chakra Two: Water

Manipura 49
Chakra Three: Fire

Anahata 67
Chakra Four: Air

Visuddha 87
Chakra Five: Sound

Ajna 109
Chakra Six: Light

Sahasrara 127
Chakra Seven: Thought

CHAKRA MEDICINE

haiku

Muladhara

Earth
Red
Having

Root Chakra

Muladhara

the life adventure
is physical, natural
beginning with breath

the right to be here
tadasana - mountain pose
survival, grounding

stillness, root support
red, solid, the sense of smell
body, food, matter

in color spectrum
red has the longest wavelength
slowest vibration

roots are nourishing
accept gravity, descend
into the body

beginning, the earth
legs, feet, bones, large intestine
teeth, the right to have

pelvic floor, coccyx
between pubis and tailbone
the base of the spine

coccygeal plexus
the lumbar vertebrae of
the spinal column

the sciatic nerve
from the sacrum to the feet
earthbound connection

ground - a powerful
nervous system connection
with earth through the feet

Muladhara

nature, creation
made up of the three *gunas*
known as *prakriti*

the three *gunas* are
tamas, *rajas* and *sattva*
the constituents

tamas - inertia
to focus and manifest
the fleshy body

the language is form
personal form is expressed
as human body

connected to source
present in the here and now
being real, solid

guts, instinct, wisdom
live humbly, simply, in grace
a true path in life

first - *Muladhara*
the body contains the soul
feel pain, get in touch

we develop pain
to show us where we resist
wholeness, so we heal

a strong foundation
builds a healthy sense of self
authenticity

when our sense of self
is embodied, less need to
affirm through ego

Muladhara

state of groundedness
decisions made easily
present enjoyment

wanting to be here
self-responsibility
caring for the self

understand body
heal body, accept body
these are challenges

limits, discipline
create within boundaries
material world

containment, to keep
magnetize material
self-worth, ownership

similarity
indrawing of the center
unity makes form

increasing value
literal, figurative
to give yourself more

healthy abundance
expecting prosperity
creativity

money, love, rest, time
develop abilities
to allow, to have

take care of yourself
listen to your body's needs
be a provider

Muladhara

your body, the earth
examine your foundation
simplification

to be embodied
love, feel, validate and heal
be secure, stable

ecological
planetary well-being
Muladhara health

gravitation is
Muladhara's principle
condensed consciousness

equivalency
materialization
unification

gravitational
field. matter and energy
drawn toward itself

the downward vortex
density and cohesion
manifestation

similar forces
in nature and direction
reach critical mass

law of attraction
matter - condensed energy
be aware of moods

bottom of chakra
column. downward moving force
gaining bulk, substance

Muladhara

forces from the top
descending through six levels
are most solid here

upward motion is
centrifugal - expansive
away from center

manifestation
is movement inward, toward
self - centripetal

being as human
physical identity
through *Muladhara*

survival response
instinctual functioning
first chakra concerns

instincts - hunger, fear
need for rest, warmth and shelter
life is survival

a body in threat
heartbeat acceleration
adrenaline rush

body in danger
sharpening of the senses
increased blood supply

chakras are filters
chakras shut down to protect
from harsh surroundings

psychic energy
can overwhelm the chakras
grounding helps release

Muladhara

'mind over matter'
integrate polarities
change this paradigm

human consciousness
embodied identity
mind within matter

form, integration
physical is personal
unite with your soul

the demon is fear
awaken *Muladhara*
roots are made from guts

unresolved conflict
feeling anxious, insecure
panic, fight or flight

over attachment
or constant change unsettle
extremes lack balance

feeling guilt, worry
scarcity mentality
let go, allow more

health and finances
reflect struggle or balance
in *Muladhara*

ungrounded culture
the body is not cherished
we develop pain

with roots ungrounded
personal and collective
progress is threatened

Muladhara

threats to survival
of self and of the planet
crisis wakes us up

damaged first chakra
living in a fantasy
apart from nature

blocked *Muladhara*
cut off from source energy
we lose our life path

trapped in chakra one
is survival consciousness
can't get off the ground

blocks - obesity
hemorrhoids, constipation
anorexia

degenerative
arthritis, sciatica
knee pain - imbalance

simple human touch
for intense physical pain
can help with grounding

massages, hot baths
heal the divorced mind-body
movement, dance, yoga

warrior three pose -
virabhadrasana III
balance, leverage

stable protection
from everyday overwhelm
alana - high lunge

Muladhara

uttanasana
a downward channel for stress
release life tension

salabasana -
half locust and full locust
strengthen back support

head to knee pose is
janu sirsasana. it
opens the hamstrings

connect with nature
bridge - *setu bhandasana*
dynamic contact

grounding inversion
viparita karani
reverse energy

from *sukhasana*
cross-legged spinal twist is
a low back release

apanasana
stressful sensations let go
into mother earth

try *padmasana*
and *pavamuktasana*
and *malasana*

food is vibration
nuts, legumes, root vegetables
for *Muladhara*

eat well, receive love
fruits of the earth grow to share
nourishment, pleasure

Muladhara

Svadhisthana

Water
Orange
Feeling

Sacral Chakra

Muladhara

two - *Svadhisthana*
vinyasa, movement in flow
the water chakra

sexuality
desire, pleasure, sweetness, taste
feel, liquid, orange

pelvic basin, womb
genitals, procreation
lower abdomen

kidney and bladder
circulatory system
to feel and to flow

blood circulation
urine elimination
and reproduction

in center between
the navel and genitals
is the 'seat of life'

corresponding to
the sacral plexus of nerves
the home of motion

sensation processed
in lower section of brain
the limbic system

hypothalamus
hormones, autonomic nerves
homeostasis

unity becomes
duality. we move from
solid to liquid

Muladhara

from earth element
to water, stillness becomes
movement, emotions

form becomes formless
water, change, polarities
nurturance, I feel

to understand self
we recognize the other
to reach out and grow

consciousness moves from
unity to difference
desire to connect

clairsentience - psychic
ability to acquire
knowledge through feeling

to be an empath
is to feel the emotions
of another soul

awareness of self
awareness of the other
must be in balance

The Book of Changes
in Chinese philosophy
I Ching. yin and yang

polaric forces
feminine and masculine
dance of change and growth

receptivity
heaven and earth and the moon
moving the ocean

Muladhara

duality seeks
to return to unity
opposites attract

Svadhisthana is
stimulated by the dance
of polarities

solid earth transforms
to infinite consciousness
it starts with movement

Muladhara holds
and creates. *Svadhisthana*
lets go and lets flow

movement is essence
Svadhisthana is life force
dance, animate, flow

flow is allowing
energetic connection
between entities

out of unity
duality is rising
seeking its return

inanimate from
animate, the difference
between life and death

shushumna channel
from coccyx to crown of head
the main *nadi* line

nadis are channels
Sanskrit for 'flowing water'
subtle energy

Muladhara

alternate channels
control yin-yang energy
moving through chakras

pingala - nadi
to the right of *shushumna*
masculine, solar

left side of the brain
controls speech, rational thought
the right side body

pingala - upward
flowing energy through right
nostril - liberty

pingala aligns
with *surya* - sun, active, yang
daytime energy

ida - to the left
of *shushumna*, feminine
nadi line, lunar

right side of the brain
creative, intuitive
the left side body

ida - energy
flows downward through left nostril
creativity

ida refers to
chandra - the moon, passive, yin
lovers in the night

yin and yang forces
spin the chakras along the
shushumna axis

Muladhara

chakras are the gears
moving subtle energy
up and down the spine

yin and yang chakras
odd numbers - yang - chakra one
foundation, begin

even numbers - yin
chakra two is receptive
feminine, the womb

desire and passion
move oceans of energy
the demon is guilt

avoiding pleasure
or overindulging both
create imbalance

to be in balance
be open to feel pleasure
without attachment

pain makes us contract
pleasure creates expansion
toward consciousness

healthy sensation
rejuvenates the spirit
psyche and body

heal relationships
personal and cultural
empathy unites

feeling is movement
emotions and energy
personal weather

Muladhara

repressing feelings
restricting movements, holding
cause chronic tension

a blocked emotion
unconscious motivations
wreak havoc in life

flow is harmony
the dance of body and mind
inner unity

sentience evolves
desire is movement is change
higher consciousness

altered awareness
kundalini is rising
up the *shushumna*

the chakra system
and *kundalini* yoga
are based in *tantra*

tantric thought - human
body as microcosm
of the universe

profane is sacred
Shakti - divine feminine
body as freedom

tantric practices
wake dormant *kundalini*
at base of the spine

Shakti energy
travels up the *shushumna*
to crown of the head

Muladhara

the crown chakra, bliss
all *nadis* flow together
supreme consciousness

divine masculine
Shiva resides at the crown
the seventh chakra

Shiva and *Shakti*
eternally making love
the divine union

sexual couple
the transcendental union
with another soul

an aura body
'the mystic child' - magical
powers called *siddhis*

clear chakras open
repressed sexuality
decreases life force

psychic energy
in excess inhibits male
and female gonads

affected by sex -
sixth chakra third eye center
the pineal gland

sexual hormones
inhibit melatonin
production - third eye

duality is
pain. sacred dance of yin and
yang restores oneness

Muladhara

bodies are sacred
senses bring ecstasy, joy
and enlightenment

body, family
tantra means 'a web or loom'
weaving existence

sex, sacred union
restore, renew, reproduce
the householder stage

maternal nature
nurturance is the essence
fundamental need

simple acts of touch
are vital to the human
for a healthy life

Svadhisthana blocks -
impotence, frigidity
lack of connection

poor circulation
low back pain, kidney troubles
leg cramps, hip stiffness

downward facing dog
and seated wide angle pose
for *Svadhisthana*

utkatasana
virabhadrasana II
bhujangasana

practice *jathara*
parivartanasana
known as maltese twist

Muladhara

seated butterfly
pose - *baddha konasana*
with a forward fold

nadhi shodhana
alternate nostril breathing
balance left - right brain

guna is *tamas*
a quality of darkness
in *Svadhisthana*

food for chakra two
liquids. nourish with water
flushing the kidneys

the path to wholeness
inspired by separation
is duality

Muladhara

Manipura

Fire
Yellow
Doing

Solar Plexus Chakra

Manipura

three - *Manipura*
solar plexus and navel
upward facing dog

yellow, sight, I can
will, power, assertiveness
laughter, joy, anger

warmth and light, plasma
digestive system, muscles
the fire element

self, autonomy
technology, energy
metabolism

psyche and soma
emerge from the unconscious
create willed action

Manipura is
the realm of activity
fire ignites action

the solar plexus
below sternum to navel
the navel chakra

sympathetic nerves
in the pit of the stomach
belly of body

the adrenal glands
produce important hormones
for regulation

metabolism
immune system, blood pressure
stress response functions

Manipura

stomach, gallbladder
small intestine and liver
spleen and pancreas

pancreas - enzymes
for digestion are produced
by exocrine glands

endocrine function
in the pancreas controls
blood sugar levels

Manipura is
metabolic energy
throughout the body

matter and movement
together are synergy
in *Manipura*

earth and water flow
downward with gravity, path
of least resistance

fire moves upward to
destroy form. transformation
a new dimension

passive elements
earth and water converted
into heat and light

prakriti transmutes
tamas to *rajas guna*
rajas is action

fire is transforming
we overcome inertia
breaking old patterns

Manipura

will liberates us -
expectations of others
addictive habits

knowing true power
action with higher purpose
easy and graceful

chakras one, two, three
mass, movement and energy
interdependence

descending current
energy into purpose
is intelligence

the sun. light and heat
self-generating cycle
nuclear fusion

Manipura means
'lustrous gem.' the spark between
Shiva and *Shakti*

the power of life
give and take of human warmth
not a cold control

Manipura - yang
to be withdrawn, cold, controlled
is a closed system

closed systems burn up
anger, self-criticism
expression is blocked

fire is dynamic
interaction with the world
fuels our vital fire

Manipura

not domination
replacing 'power over'
with 'power within'

enhance, empower
strengthen rather than threaten
cooperation

combine, integrate
do not fight or dominate
incorporation

power outside self
a submissive paradigm
parents, teachers, boss

disempowering
a set of obligations
rather than choices

doing what you're told
is to give your will away
go deeper, be true

maintain inner will
social cooperation
requires consciousness

to lose connection
destructive behavior with
drugs and alcohol

caught up in something
negative - create stillness
refuse this motion

to assimilate
adjust actions to achieve
highest potential

Manipura

memory, knowledge
to imagine and create
beyond here and now

enthusiasm
liberate and find freedom
in autonomy

Manipura is
consciously controlled change, choice
personal power

to direct desire
is to create our future
give up victimhood

create momentum
lasting change will only come
from our own efforts

a strong sense of self
trust in your own volition
daring use of will

beyond the ego
self responsibility
service to the world

openness to flow
graceful purpose, alignment
practical level

in touch with desire
we are able to engage
knowing what you want

choose the big picture
discipline is important
focus attention

Manipura

the larger purpose
transcends our fleeting feelings
when our will is fixed

within mystery
far reaching cause and effect
lies our real purpose

be in harmony
personal and divine will
greater cosmic will

shame is the demon
we must feel we have something
to give to others

to break inertia
awaken *Manipura*
give up being safe

risk, success, failure
realistic sense of self
self esteem is born

communication
of the interior self
we receive feedback

love and acceptance
third and fourth chakras unite
in relationships

misunderstanding
avoid invalidation
from those who can't see

let it go, release
when something is not working
break the attachment

Manipura

straining with effort -
stop. strong opposition - stop.
resistance is fear

anger - blocked power
not worth damaging loved ones
work it out within

do you project blame?
find wholeness, satisfaction
release resentment

love feeds energy
from upper chakras into
Manipura, strength

focused energy
successful relationships
exhilaration

laughter is power
be accepting of yourself
and situations

be noncritical
take life less seriously
find a new outcome

direct attention
energy will follow to
manifest power

imbalances are
tight hard stomach, large belly
sunken diaphragm

ulcers, digestive
disorders, diabetes
hypoglycemic

Manipura

thrill-seeking is a
behavioral imbalance
in *Manipura*

try *prasarita
padottanasana* to
stabilize your core

*trikonasana
paschimottanasana
dhanurasana*

try *parivrtta
parsvakonasana* to
ignite chakra three

navasana - pike
pose. *matsyendrasana* -
seated spinal twist

for *Manipura*
eat starches, metabolize
food is energy

sugar addiction
a third chakra imbalance
avoid stimulants

unprocessed whole grains
are slowly and thoroughly
assimilated

empower yourself
take responsibility
own your energy

self-esteem is the
foundation for opening
Anahata - heart

Manipura

Anahata

Air
Green
Loving

Heart Chakra

Anahata

Anahata, heart
its meaning - 'unstruck' - I love
compassion, touch, green

within and without
the spiritual center
above and below

outer state - gaseous
body parts - lungs, arms, hands, heart
pericardium

cardiac plexus
and pulmonary plexus
heart, lungs, thymus gland

the thymus gland rests
on the heart, training T cells
for immunity

circulatory
system mastered by the heart
transports oxygen

breath is life-giving
purifying energy
loving in essence

air, relationship
affinity, unity
breath, balance, healing

inner peace, wholeness
midpoint of chakra system
the center of love

Shiva and *Shakti*
unify *Anahata*
a state of being

Anahata

divine empathy
is presence that radiates
love and compassion

love does not depend
on outside stimulation
in *Anahata*

needs have been fulfilled
sex and passion transcended
a deep sense of peace

joyful acceptance
of our place among all life
inner harmony

Anahata - sound
made without two things striking
unhurt, fresh and clean

the demon is grief
innocence is radiance
release fights, old hurts

equilibrium
love within complexity
equanimity

element is air
expansive and spirited
freedom and softness

air represents breath
prana - vital energy
creating all life

control of the breath
the tool for transformation
body and spirit

Anahata

interface between
physical and mental worlds
breath is influence

the integrator
between upper and lower
chakras is the heart

opening the heart
is understanding that life
is relationships

balance. mind-body
inner-outer, self-other
giving-receiving

things drawn together
love is unifying force
parts become a whole

loosen boundaries
merging into ecstasy
transcending ego

accepting others
to invite love offer it
appreciation

love and approval
basic to personal growth
feelings of safety

love allows freedom
coherence at the center
creates space for change

understanding love
is self-perpetuating
expands horizons

Anahata

love is infinite
oneness, interdependence
the abundant source

loving energy
flow is blocked by jealousy
undue attachment

disintegration
rejection is human fear
threatening balance

non-love used against
ourselves is self-destructive
cut-off, separate

to live without love
may feel easier than risk
sharing and failing

fear as gatekeeper
feeling vulnerable and
protective at heart

too much restriction
creates alienation
within self and world

breaking negative
cycles is letting go of
withholding patterns

all chakras function
to create and maintain love
feel and understand

heart chakra is yin
let things be the way they are
profound love allows

Anahata

fundamental truth
connection with all of life
mundane is sacred

gravitation and
radiation. love keeps us
in relationship

binds without limits
eternal stabilizer
closeness and distance

spirit connection
realize no boundaries
we are all essence

the web of oneness
joining all relationships
is made of pure love

awareness. concepts
patterns, structure, perception
communication

patterns that last are
in dynamic symmetry
parts become a whole

coalescence of
matter and information
is relationship

self-composedness
chakras receive energy
from the *shushumna*

balanced within self
we enter the mandala
of life whole-hearted

Anahata

grace has stepping stones
enduring relationships
are in harmony

in love we give up
individuality
to be in union

exhilarating
love can lift us off our feet
we must be grounded

we must retain self
transcend our separateness
in a balanced way

the art of being
in balance is elegant
gentle, delicate

true love flows freely
in a synchronistic dance
between heart centers

love is not attached
it is a state of being
harmony with self

love is natural
believe it is around you
in all things always

affinity means
to enter into and be
in combination

an intrinsic fit
within atomic structure
coming together

Anahata

chemistry, bonding
each has something the other
is lacking, to merge

love projects outward
what you seek is seeking you
matching energy

self-acceptance is
first unconditional love
we give what we have

we radiate love
from inner togetherness
we have created

tune into heartbeat
tune into resonance with
core rhythm of life

Anahata is
the ultimate healing force
love is to make whole

energy channels
carry energy from heart
through arms to the hands

hands are sensitive
far more neural receptors
sensory organs

create and receive
hands are tools of perception
psychic energy

realize oneness
non-judgmental compassion
for others, reach out

Anahata

true healers tune in
aligned, balanced, open, they
are presence of love

it is our vision
of harmony and balance
that inspires others

the environment
restores an organism
or situation

remaining grounded
the healer is catalyst
we each heal ourselves

heart chakra problems
high blood pressure, heart disease
lung disease, asthma

cat-cow, camel, fish
heart-opening *asanas*
dolphin and rabbit

bhujangasana
ardha bhujangasana -
cobra and sphinx pose

revolved head to knee
parivrtta means revolved
heart opens skyward

variation of
virabhadrasana II
reverse warrior

pranayama is
a system of yoga built
on breathing techniques

Anahata

oxygen, air, breath
release toxins, emotions
change body and mind

breath creates our voice
free up the chest, upper back
help deepen the breath

Anahata is
rajas and *sattva gunas*
passion and wisdom

food for chakra four
Anahata thrives on greens
plant-based, vegetables

healing is balance
opening the heart chakra
creates connection

Anahata

Visuddha

Sound
Blue
Speaking

Throat Chakra

Visuddha

Visuddha is sound
chakra five, the throat chakra
purification

sound and hearing, space
ideas into symbols
synthesis, I speak

vagus nerve controls
throat sensation, swallowing
and voice production

vocal chords, tongue, mouth
create speech through cranial
nerves in the brainstem

Visuddha relates
to pharyngeal plexus
of nerves in the throat

neck, shoulders, arms, hands
vibration, blue and bright blue
creativity

communication
sound, rhythm, harmonics, words
self-expression, yang

coordinating
extension of consciousness
between entities

connecting all life
requires communication
civilization

complex tasks of life
cooperative culture
shares information

Visuddha

DNA, hormones
brain waves and muscle tissues
all communicate

creation through sound
dynamic, synthesizing
transmit and receive

listening, speaking
writing, chanting and language
art and oracles

symbolic nature
represent perceived patterns
access inner planes

climb to chakra five
away from the physical
the world in symbols

communication
is physical transcendence
beyond the body

bodily limits
physical borders diffuse
ascending chakras

boundaries around
conscious thought experience
are impossible

communication
is a unifying act
we extend ourselves

information from
one brain is accessible
to another brain

Visuddha

expansion. our world
becomes larger through shared thought
making connections

beyond our limits
the ascending current of
consciousness unites

descending chakras
thought patterns made specific
through naming process

naming focuses
to name is to clarify
it is this not that

structure and meaning
give shape to reality
creating the world

energy moving
both up and down *shushumna*
communication

Visuddha is the
gateway between dimensions
of body and mind

cerulean blue
the neck and shoulder region
called the throat chakra

the mediator
between abstract ideas
and the manifest

purification
to open and access the
Visuddha chakra

Visuddha

sound as vibration
a force inherent in all
is purifying

cellular structure
of matter is affected
by nature of sound

the subtle body
dissonant frequencies are
harmonized by sound

Visuddha and the
upper chakras require more
sensitivity

akasha - spirit
element is ether - sky
the etheric plane

world of vibrations
aura, sound, the subtle plane
nuanced impressions

metaphysical
systems - earth, water, fire, air
the four elements

a fifth element
universal element
ether - spirit - space

the four elements
the physical world. the fifth
non-physical realm

Visuddha is last
assigned element. ether
shares top three chakras

Visuddha

climb up *shushumna*
each plane vibrates higher, more
efficient, faster

manifestation
of rhythm is vibration
impact, cymatics

natural patterns
are produced in mediums
when sound waves project

OM is the whole world
the basic emanation
creating matter

matter vibrates. this
movement is how we perceive
matter's emptiness

vibration - rhythm
a repeated, regular
pattern of movement

turning of seasons
diurnal rhythms - day/night
cycles of the moon

movement of the breath
the beating of hearts. life is
being in rhythm

tune our consciousness
into subtle vibrations
of the universe

respond to the tone
bring conscious awareness to
actions on this plane

Visuddha

notice vibrations
people and situations
if something is off

resonant rhythm
is often lacking in life
at odds with the world

carried vibrations
within our minds and bodies
make a difference

a calm, centered state
affects cellular level
thoughts, moves, emotions

all sounds are wave forms
sympathetic vibration
rhythm entrainment

resonance is when
two wave forms 'lock into phase'
the exact same rate

result of two waves
combining same frequency
increased amplitude

increased amplitude
increased energy, volume
more power and depth

cultures are entrained
environments influence
neighbors, friends and peers

inner vibrations
affected - billboards, social
pressure, pollution

Visuddha

people in households
are entrained to each other
subtle vibrations

psychological
and physiological
subconscious level

body movements of
listener and speaker are
synchronized with voice

misunderstanding
before entrainment occurs
we need resonance

with entrainment we
experience connection
healthy frequencies

beneath illusion
when we truly resonate
affects us deeply

we choose vibrations
good or bad, in harmony
or disharmony

actions, thoughts, eating
emotions, environment
vibrate the chakras

mantras are sacred
sounds used in meditation
and chanting. magic

mantras change our thoughts
and emotions into a
pure graceful pattern

Visuddha

we transcend random
mind fragments and perceive the
wholeness of being

rhythms created
by mantra meditation
influence the world

the *bija* mantras
universe is made of sound
each chakra - seed sound

Muladhara seed -
LAM. *Svadhisthana* seed - VAM
Manipura - RAM

Anahata - YAM
Visuddha - HAM. *Ajna* - OM
Sahasrara - (none)

M is maternal
material. A - father
non-material

consonants are hard
material, while vowels
are spiritual

uttering mantras
controls mind-body rhythm
engaging spirit

telepathy, art
well-developed *Visuddha*
allows a new sense

consciousness is not
verbal. we translate thoughts in
symbolic structure

Visuddha

in the translation
communication essence
often distorted

through refinement and
attention to vibration
access unity

creativity
is a form of expression
chakras two and five

the artist - always
engaged with present moment
future history

creation process
art, inner discovery
we become channels

media controls
the collective consciousness
for better or worse

kind society
must expect integrity
from those in control

the demon is lies
overcoming ignorance
transforms the culture

malfunctions - stiff neck
sore throat, colds, thyroid problems
and hearing problems

balance *Visuddha*
ujjayi pranayama -
victorious breath

Visuddha

shoulder stand, plow pose
ardha uttanasana
four-legged table

matsyasana
utthita hastasana
seated spinal twist

guna is *rajas*
mutable, harmonizing
communicative

clean, nonviolent
dropping to earth when ripe, eat
fruits for *Visuddha*

purification
Visuddha, resonance with
truth enlightens us

Visuddha

Ajna

Light
Indigo + Violet
Seeing

Third Eye Chakra

Ajna

Ajna, the third eye
to perceive and to command
eyes, intuition

midpoint of the brow
carotid plexus of nerves
the base of the skull

images, I see
full self-realization
light, color, vision

imagination
and visualization
clairvoyance, seeing

shape and form distilled
indigo and violet
light waves map the world

the pineal gland
light meter for the body
'the seat of the soul'

autonomic nerves
translate light variations
hormone messages

melatonin is
triggered by light exposure
in pineal gland

it reduces stress
strengthens our immune system
slows aging process

low melatonin
levels found in depression
high in manic state

Ajna

native plants known to
induce visions - similar
to melatonin

vibrant consciousness
illusion is the demon
shadows weaving light

images and dreams
arise from the unconscious
connect us to soul

insight. guidance through
situations and darkness
intuitive light

the gift of seeing
both inner and outer worlds
essence of *Ajna*

memory of past
imagining the future
Ajna transcends time

brow chakra - third eye
psychic, etheric organ
between our two eyes

visual thinking
wisdom is interior
the internal screen

take in images
and visualization
perceive and command

to hold an image
in mind boosts its creative
real-life potential

Ajna

with interference
visualizations don't
always manifest

yin and yang *nadis*
ida and *pingala* meet
at the third eye point

develop, open
sixth chakra element - light
how much we can see

psychic perception
and eyesight acuity
inner and outer

psychic perception
auras and chakras, details
of the astral plane

natural eyesight
our visual perceptions
must be translated

we become mental
leave time-space limitations
for transpersonal

chakra six - higher
faster vibration than sound
in visible light

light travels fastest
wave packets called photons are
what constitute light

speed of light distorts
travel at the speed of light
time would cease to pass

Ajna

Ajna transcends time
Visuddha transcends distance
beyond physical

quality of light
is electromagnetic
color is the form

variations in
frequency - we discover
different colors

photon energy
hot - reds, oranges, yellows
lower frequency

in cooler colors
greens, blues, violets - photons
have more energy

red is aggressive
anger, blood and beginnings
heart, nervous system

the effect of blue
on most people - feeling peace
and tranquility

full sunlight helps heal
mood, arthritis, cancer and
other diseases

negative effect
on health and state of mind found
in fluorescent lights

bathing a person
in colored light for healing
red for exhaustion

Ajna

treatments of blue light
relief from sciatica
and inflammation

golden-orange for
diabetes. yellow for
mental clarity

visualizing
positively is treatment
at subtle level

disease is subtle
treatment at subtle level
with things like color

beauty and color
in visualization
self-healing method

examine colors
reading of our own chakras
clothing, home decor

for weaker chakras
immerse yourself in colors
that will empower

ninety percent of
information in sighted
person - through the eyes

information is
visible - intensity
location, color

patterns are defined
in spatial relationships
form in size and shape

Ajna

it is not our eyes
but our minds that see movement
and our behavior

along optic nerves
electrical impulses
meaningful patterns

it is not objects
we see but light reflected
the spaces between

psychic reception
projected imagery
life as hologram

development of
psychic abilities is
most significant

to be clairvoyant
look in spaces that are clear
fields of energy

look not at objects
relationships not things. see
the world as a whole

looking is action
internalization of
image is seeing

deeper perception
see what you choose to look at
with understanding

universal mind
the bank of holographic
memory for all

Ajna

clairvoyance - data
from the common holograph
is intuited

precognition is
'seeing' of future events
a gifted psychic

remote viewing is
to 'see' things in another
place. also a gift

we transcend time in
the sixth chakra. both future
and past are called forth

ability to
retrieve, create and project
on the mental screen

we have access to
infinite images by
infinite brain waves

ask the right questions
infinite intelligence
will provide answers

practice and patience
an open and quiet mind
to retrieve data

learning to focus
creating one-pointedness
for a deeper look

malfunctions - blindness
headaches, nightmares, blurred vision
ocular eye strain

Ajna

balance *Ajna* with
*asana - setu bandha
sarvangasana*

vrksasana - tree
vajra mudra asana
sirsana prep

the pose - *jathara
parivartanasana*
with the head centered

forehead to the floor
in *balasana* - child's pose
softening your gaze

guna is *sattva*
universality and
luminosity

sixth, seventh chakras
mind-altering substances
and fasting nourish

emptying the mind
through meditation allows
one to better see

Ajna

Sahasrara

Thought
Violet to White
Knowing

Crown Chakra

Sahasrara

Sahasrara, bliss
chakra seven, crown chakra
the top of the head

violet to white
thousandfold, understanding
consciousness, knowing

'thousandfold' - lotus
flower petals' infinite
endless unfolding

one hundred million
sensory receptors, ten
trillion synapses

the nervous system
is the receiver within
the human body

cerebral cortex
the central nervous system
thought, information

the master chakra
master gland of endocrine
pituitary

regulates hormones
for growth, reproduction and
metabolism

relates to the brain
physiologically
cerebral cortex

brains are limitless
instruments of awareness
within the body

Sahasrara

to know, immanence
understanding, to transcend
through meditation

cosmic consciousness
profound divine source of all
manifestation

an essence supreme
the underlying order
ruling principle

in the unconscious
the wisdom of the body
is *Sahasrara*

in the conscious mind
intellect, belief system
is *Sahasrara*

in superconscious
awareness of the divine
is *Sahasrara*

the blooming lotus
ultimate liberation
where we find meaning

the song of our soul
born of earthbound roots grown deep
sings into the sky

to reach this level
seeds grow upward through water
fire, air, sound and light

in pure consciousness
experience now through the
element of thought

Sahasrara

Sahasrara is
the seat of enlightenment
in yogic practice

pratyahara
means to withdraw the senses
for mental stillness

senses as gateway
in *tantric* philosophy
to *Sahasrara*

in chakra theory
it is both inner stillness
and stimulation

intelligence yields
information, withdrawal
allows pure knowledge

function is knowing
thought is unmeasurable
field of consciousness

crown chakra reaches
into infinite body
of information

information is
channeled through each chakra for
manifestation

mind as theater
we witness our thought drama
in *Sahasrara*

this thought enactment
informs our belief systems
to create meaning

Sahasrara

knowledge is received
and assimilated from
internal landscape

beyond time and space
a non-local dimension
exists within us

each chakra is a
dimension of smaller and
faster vibration

crown chakra - a plane
beyond speed, without wavelength
is omnipresence

the world in patterns
and symbols occupying
no physical space

conception is the
genesis of creation
the world in our heads

pattern is born of
concept, manifestation
infuses substance

we look at nature
the celestial universe
pattern is order

'pater' means father
pattern relates to *Shiva*
he provides the form

'mater' means mother
Shakti's raw energy makes
the material

Sahasrara

the world will show us
what our consciousness looks like
nature and man-made

crown chakra perceives
organizing principles
as meta-patterns

cosmic consciousness
universal expansion
unifying truths

at *Sahasrara*
far away from time, space and
material world

complete awareness
gateway to worlds beyond worlds
in eternity

versatility
a state of liberation
without dimension

through *Sahasrara*
Shiva's divine energy
enters the body

pure unmanifest
consciousness is *purusha*
in yogic practice

polar opposite
of *purusha* - *prakriti*
nature, creation

Shakti - *prakriti*
resides in *Muladhara*
Shiva - *purusha*

Sahasrara

known as 'the witness'
in the mystery of self
our own awareness

if we want to change
we must learn to fathom the
mystery of life

self is defined by
possession of consciousness
within the cosmos

self is a storehouse
memories, belief systems
new capacities

each life has meaning
in this way, all lives connect
pattern has purpose

individual
is linked to universal
unity, yoga

the search for meaning
basic drive of crown chakra
organization

we discern meaning
in situations to know
how to operate

consciousness is a
force of unity. design
and intelligence

inherent in all
the ordering principle
the eternal dance

Sahasrara

Shakti and *Shiva*
manifest and liberate
consciousness nature

open awareness
notice where attention goes
focus or expand

consciousness descends
to become concrete useful
manifestation

consciousness expands
to travel outward towards
abstract planes of thought

orientation
in cognitive consciousness
things, relationships

orientation
in transcendent consciousness
meta-awareness

cognitive thought is
logical. transcendent thought
is beyond logic

to perceive higher
order requires distance from
the particular

emptying the mind
focuses our awareness
we see what remains

enlightenment is
progressive understanding
in wholeness is love

Sahasrara

we create matrix
structures from experience
beliefs, principles

inner and outer
experiences maintain
cohesion this way

a trap of the mind -
our inner matrix rejects
new information

how to discern truth
how to expand consciousness
in meditation

when we meditate
we let go of old beliefs
reset the matrix

the practice allows
an evolving personal
paradigm for growth

qualities of mind
exist independently
of the perceiver

morphogenetic
fields - a theory - universe
functions by habit

the repetition
of these habits creates a
pattern over time

the pattern creates
a field. once formed, it dictates
future worldly forms

Sahasrara

when large numbers of
people hold a shared belief
their field is stronger

to change consciousness
we must tap into the field
that created it

to change a worldview
the matrix of collective
consciousness is mined

collective journey
self-conscious evolution
unite in this way

the crossroads between
finite and infinite is
moral and holy

transcendental bliss
Sahasrara chakra is
universal love

two currents exist
transcendent and immanent
liberate, create

characteristic
quality of transcendence
emptiness. let go

emptiness of mind
beyond the ordinary
no separation

liberation from
illusion and attachment
is bliss and freedom

Sahasrara

ascending current
liberation. descending
current, enjoyment

divine consciousness
enters the body, descends
gives meaning to life

Sahasrara, the
origin of all and the
gateway to beyond

guna is *sattva*
truth, peace and serenity
in *Sahasrara*

demon - attachment
false identification
pain and suffering

malfunctions - boredom
apathy and depression
alienation

other malfunctions
are an inability
to learn, confusion

savasana and
seated meditation will
balance crown chakra

psychological
effects of meditation
well-being and peace

we are the vortex
find center, understanding
in meditation

Sahasrara

immanence is the
awareness of the divine
within each of us

transcendence is the
awareness of the divine
without, all around

true self knowledge is
understanding inner and
outer worlds as one

enlightenment is
not knowing all the answers
it is the questions

Sahasrara

www.ingramcontent.com/pod-product-compliance
Lightning Source LLC
Chambersburg PA
CBHW031322160426
43196CB00007B/627